ANY VOICE
COMBINATION

MW00668781

Classics for Two

10 Masterwork Duets
from the Renaissance through the Romantic Era

COMPILED AND EDITED BY PATRICK M. LIEBERGEN

Table of Contents

	Page	CD Track
Foreword	3	
Ave Maria	4	1
Giulio Caccini (1545–1618)		
Laudamus te	14	2
Antonio Vivaldi (1678–1741)		
Sweet Nymph, Come to Thy Lover	24	3
Thomas Morley (c. 1557–1602)		
Deh prendi un dolce amplesso		
(Ah, Let Me Hold You Closely)	31	4
Wolfgang Amadeus Mozart (1756–1791)		
Pachelbel's Canon of Peace	34	5
Johann Pachelbel (1653–1706)		
Let's Imitate Her Notes Above	40	6
George Frideric Handel (1685–1750)		
Sonntagsmorgen *(This Day I Praise the Lord)*	52	7
Felix Mendelssohn (1809–1847)		
Panis angelicus *(O Lord, I Pray to Thee)*	57	8
César Franck (1822–1890)		
Sing with Festive Cheer	62	9
Antonio Salieri (1750–1825)		
When at Night I Go to Sleep		
(Abends, will ich schlafen gehn)	70	10
Engelbert Humperdinck (1854–1921)		
Optional Instrumental Accompaniments	74	
Editor's Notes	92	
Pronunciation Guides	97	

Classics for Two accompaniment tracks were recorded at Red Rock Recording in Saylorsburg, PA.

Sally K. Albrecht, Piano • Kent Heckman, Engineer

Book (27108)	ISBN-10: 0-7390-4388-9	ISBN-13: 978-0-7390-4388-2
Book/CD (27110)	ISBN-10: 0-7390-4389-7	ISBN-13: 978-0-7390-4389-9
Accompaniment CD (27109)	ISBN-10: 0-7390-4390-0	ISBN-13: 978-0-7390-4390-5

Cover Art: Pablo Picasso (Spanish, 1881–1973)
The Lovers, 1923
Oil on linen, 130.2 x 97.2 cm.
© The National Gallery of Art, Chester Dale Collection 1963.10.192

About the artist: Known as a rebel in the art world, Pablo Picasso (born in Málaga, Spain on October 25, 1881) is now recognized as one of the most influential and recognized geniuses in art history. In his youth, he experimented with many different styles and went through several different periods ("Blue Period," "Rose Period"), but later was known for developing his own style called Cubism. In the 1920's, he produced work in a neoclassical style, like the painting featured on this cover. He spent much of his life traveling between Paris and his native Spain, and, in his later years, also occupied himself with sculpture, pottery, and print-making. He died in Mougins, France, on April 8, 1973.

Foreword

Classics for Two features ten duets brought together for the first time in one collection. Representing a wide range of styles and composers, these selections from the Renaissance, Classic, and Romantic eras are presented with historical information and suggestions for performance. Additionally, pronunciation guides are included for all songs with non-English texts. Selected, edited and arranged by Patrick M. Liebergen, this valuable collection is an indispensable resource for duet singing.

The preparation of this anthology involved a number of editorial considerations. Original scores were consulted in the preparation of the editions when possible, and any changes are noted in the editor's comments for each selection beginning on page 92. If instrumental accompaniments were included in the original scores, then the keyboard accompaniments in this edition are reductions of those parts. Separate instrumental parts for the performance of seven selections are included beginning on page 74.

The editor has also provided transliterations for the pronunciation of all foreign language texts on pages 97–99. While the pronunciation guides are a helpful resource, they cannot replace the experience and expertise of a professional vocal coach or music teacher.

Classics for Two is available with or without compact disc recordings of the accompaniments. These accompaniments, masterfully recorded by Sally K. Albrecht, may be useful for both rehearsal and performance.

Acknowledgements

I would like to thank Sally K. Albrecht, my editor at Alfred Publishing Company, for her excellent suggestions in the preparation of this anthology and for her outstanding piano performance on the Accompaniment CDs. I would also like to express my gratitude to Dr. Daniel Newman of the University of Wisconsin-Eau Claire for his review of my pronunciation guides.

Patrick M. Liebergen
April, 2007

Patrick M. Liebergen

Patrick M. Liebergen is widely published as a choral editor, arranger and composer of masterwork vocal and choral editions, collections and cantatas, as well as original choral works. The Director of Choral Activities as the University of Wisconsin-Stout in Menomonie, Wisconsin, Dr. Liebergen has served in a variety of positions as a leader of school and church music. With music degrees from St. Norbert College in DePere, WI, the University of Wisconsin-Madison, and the University of Colorado-Boulder, he frequently appears throughout the country as an adjudicator and clinician. Dr. Liebergen has received choral composition awards from the Twin Cities Church Musicians' Association, the Wisconsin Choral Directors' Association, and ASCAP, and his works have been performed by choirs around the world.

Sally K. Albrecht

The piano performances on the Accompaniment CDs are by Sally K. Albrecht. Sally is the Director of School Choral Publications for Alfred Publishing. She is a popular choral conductor, composer, and clinician, and has degrees in Music and Theater from Rollins College and an M.A. in Drama and Accompanying from the University of Miami.

1. Ave Maria

with optional flute

Text setting and Arrangement by
PATRICK M. LIEBERGEN

Music by
GIULIO CACCINI (1545-1618)

Flute part is on pages 74-75.

27108

ve Ma - ri - a.

ve Ma - ri - a.

A - - -

A - - -

2. Laudamus te

(We Praise You, Lord)

English words by
PATRICK M. LIEBERGEN

from *GLORIA*
Music by **ANTONIO VIVALDI** (1678-1741)
Edited and arranged by **PATRICK M. LIEBERGEN**

103

3. Sweet Nymph, Come to Thy Lover

with optional keyboard accompaniment and two flutes

Additional words and Arrangement by
PATRICK M. LIEBERGEN

Music by
THOMAS MORLEY (c. 1557-1602)

Flute parts are on pages 76-77.

27108

4. Deh prendi un dolce amplesso
(Ah, Let Me Hold You Closely)

Italian words by **CATERINO MAZZOLÀ** (1745-1806)
English Words by **PATRICK M. LIEBERGEN**

from LA CLEMENZA DI TITO
Music by **WOLFGANG AMADEUS MOZART** (1756-1791)
Edited by **PATRICK M. LIEBERGEN**

5. Pachelbel's Canon of Peace

with optional flute

Latin setting by
PATRICK M. LIEBERGEN

from *CANON IN D*
by **JOHANN PACHELBEL** (1653-1706)
Edited and arranged by **PATRICK M. LIEBERGEN**

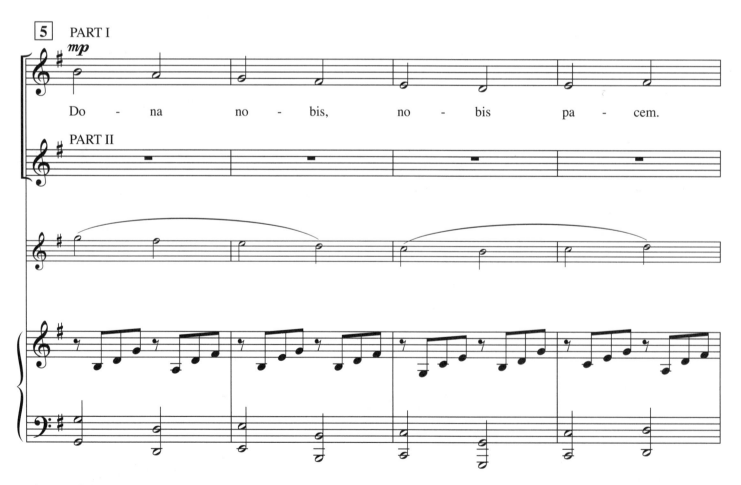

Flute or C-instrument part is on page 78.

27108

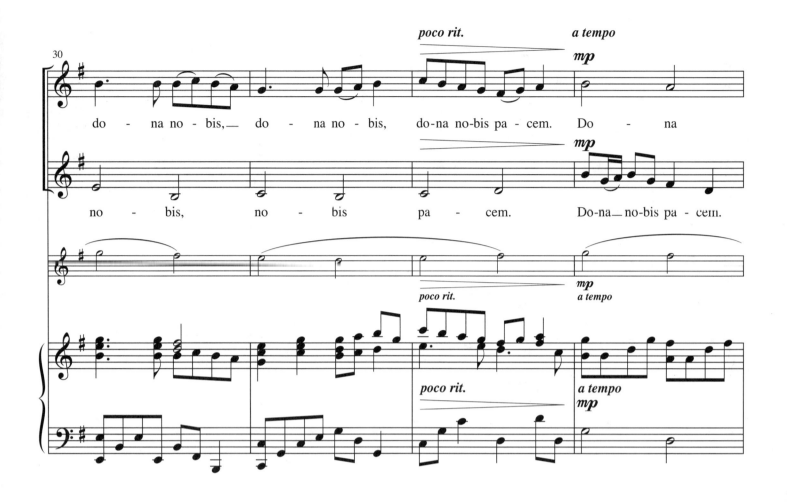

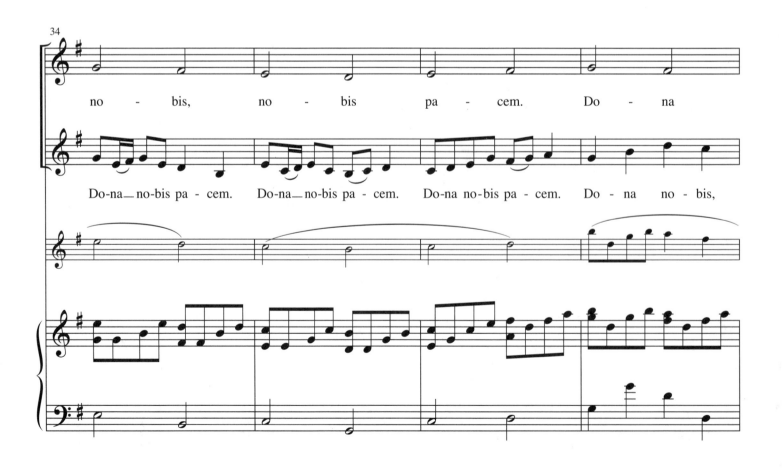

6. Let's Imitate Her Notes Above

with optional two violins and cello

Words by **NEWBURGH HAMILTON** (1712-1759)

from *ALEXANDER'S FEAST OR THE POWER OF MUSIC*
Music by **GEORGE FRIDERIC HANDEL** (1685-1750)
Edited by **PATRICK M. LIEBERGEN**

Violin and cello parts are on pages 80-85.

im - i - tate___ her notes___ a - bove!   And may this eve - ning

And may this eve - ning

ev - - er prove   sa - cred to Har -

ev - - er prove   sa - cred to Har -

cred_____ to Love._____

cred_____ to Love._____

7. Sonntagsmorgen
(This Day I Praise the Lord)

German words by
JOHANN LUDWIG UHLAND (1787-1862)
English words by **PATRICK M. LIEBERGEN**

Op. 77, No. 1
Music by **FELIX MENDELSSOHN** (1809-1847)
Edited by **PATRICK M. LIEBERGEN**

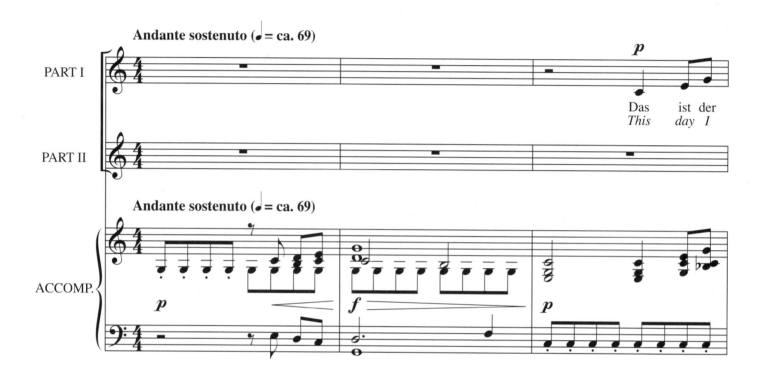

8. Panis angelicus
(O Lord, I Pray to Thee)
with optional flute and cello

English words by
PATRICK M. LIEBERGEN

from *Messe à 3 voix*
Music by **CÉSAR FRANCK** (1822-1890)
Edited and arranged by **PATRICK M. LIEBERGEN**

Flute and cello parts are on pages 86-87.

27108

9. Sing with Festive Cheer

with optional two flutes

Words by
PATRICK M. LIEBERGEN

from *LES DANAIDES*
Music by **ANTONIO SALIERI** (1750-1825)
Edited and Arranged by
PATRICK M. LIEBERGEN

Flute parts are on pages 88-91.

27108

Sing we to-day for all to hear,
(we Now - ell)

Sing we to-day, O sing for all to hear,
(we Now - ell,)

Al - le - lu - ia, al - le - lu, al - le - lu - ia!

Al - le - lu - ia, al - le - lu, al - le - lu - ia!

Sing we to-day with fes - tive cheer,
(we Now - ell)

Sing we to-day, O sing with fes - tive cheer,
(we Now - ell,)

sing____ we to - day with fes - tive cheer!
(we Now - ell)

sing____ we to - day with fes - tive____ cheer!
(we Now - ell)

song, to - geth - er all re - joice!

song, to - geth - er all re - joice!

Re - joice!
(Now - ell!)

Re - joice!
(Now - ell!)

10. When at Night I Go to Sleep
(Abends, will ich schlafen gehn)

German words by **ADELHEIDE WETTE** (1858-1916)
English words by **CONSTANCE BACHE** (1846-1903)

from *HÄNSEL UND GRETEL*
Music by **ENGELBERT HUMPERDINCK** (1854-1921)
Arranged by **PATRICK M. LIEBERGEN**

guide my steps to Heav - en.
Him - mels Pa - ra - die - sen!

steps to heav - en.
Him - mel wei - sen!

FLUTE (or C-Instrument)

1. Ave Maria

GIULIO CACCINI (1546-1618)
Arranged by **PATRICK M. LIEBERGEN**

FLUTE I (or C-Instrument)

3. Sweet Nymph, Come to Thy Lover

Music by
THOMAS MORLEY (c. 1557-1602)
Arranged by **PATRICK M. LIEBERGEN**

FLUTE II (or C-Instrument)

3. Sweet Nymph, Come to Thy Lover

Music by
THOMAS MORLEY (c. 1557-1602)
Arranged by **PATRICK M. LIEBERGEN**

27108

FLUTE (or C-Instrument)

5. Pachelbel's Canon of Peace

from *CANON IN D*
by **JOHANN PACHELBEL** (1653-1706)
Edited and arranged by **PATRICK M. LIEBERGEN**

6. Let's Imitate Her Notes Above

from *ALEXANDER'S FEAST OR THE POWER OF MUSIC*
Music by **GEORGE FRIDERIC HANDEL** (1685-1750)
Edited by **PATRICK M. LIEBERGEN**

VIOLIN I

6. Let's Imitate Her Notes Above

VIOLIN II

from *ALEXANDER'S FEAST OR THE POWER OF MUSIC*
Music by **GEORGE FRIDERIC HANDEL** (1685-1750)
Edited by **PATRICK M. LIEBERGEN**

6. Let's Imitate Her Notes Above

CELLO

from *ALEXANDER'S FEAST OR THE POWER OF MUSIC*
Music by **GEORGE FRIDERIC HANDEL** (1685-1750)
Edited by **PATRICK M. LIEBERGEN**

8. Panis angelicus
(O Lord, I Pray to Thee)

FLUTE (or C-Instrument)

from *Messe à 3 voix*
by **CÉSAR FRANCK** (1822-1890)
Edited and arranged by **PATRICK M. LIEBERGEN**

8. Panis angelicus
(O Lord, I Pray to Thee)

CELLO

from *Messe à 3 voix*
by **CÉSAR FRANCK** (1822-1890)
Edited and arranged by **PATRICK M. LIEBERGEN**

9. Sing with Festive Cheer

FLUTE I

from LES DANAIDES
Music by **ANTONIO SALIERI** (1750-1825)
Edited and Arranged by
PATRICK M. LIEBERGEN

Words by
PATRICK M. LIEBERGEN

9. Sing with Festive Cheer

FLUTE II

from *LES DANAIDES*
Music by **ANTONIO SALIERI** (1750-1825)
Edited and Arranged by
PATRICK M. LIEBERGEN

Words by
PATRICK M. LIEBERGEN

Editor's Notes

1. Ave Maria
Giulio Caccini (1545–1618)

Page 4

Giulio Caccini was a highly successful song composer as well as a singer, voice teacher and instrumentalist in Italy in the early part of the Baroque era. His musical career began in Rome as a singer in the Cappela Giulia. He was later recruited to work in Florence, where he remained to sing, teach and compose music for the Medici court.

Caccini eventually became famous for developing a new style of solo song, which involved a declamatory setting of the words, a musical sensitivity to the structure of the text, and a flexible approach to rhythm and tempo. This new type of song, called monody, included the performance of ornaments written out on the score, accompanied by a simple basso continuo. Since the bass part was to be harmonized in an improvisatory manner on another instrument, Caccini included a shorthand method of figures on the score to indicate which harmonies were to be played.

Caccini published his first collection of songs, *Le nuove musiche*, in 1602 and his second collection, *Nuove musiche e nuova maniera di scriverle*, in 1614. His first publication consisted of madrigals and airs for solo voice with basso continuo that he had written in the previous twenty years of his life.

Caccini's beautiful "Ave Maria" has become one of his most beloved solo works in recent years. This arrangement is available for performance by S.A.T.B. (21042), T.T.B.B. (22963), S.A.B. (20143) and 2-part (20144) voices, published by Alfred Publishing Company.

2. Laudamus te
Antonio Vivaldi (1678–1741)

Page 14

Antonio Vivaldi was a renowned composer and violin virtuoso in Venice, Italy, during the Baroque era. Born into a family of musicians, he studied composition and violin before becoming a Roman Catholic priest. He then devoted his musical talents to teaching orphaned girls at the Conservatory of the Pieta in Venice, where he conducted Saturday and Sunday evening concerts of his music. Often called the "prete rosse" ("red priest") because of his hair, his fame soon spread for his musical talents as a composer and violinist. Due to ill health and problems with the church authorities concerning his behavior as a priest, he left the active service of the priesthood, devoting all of his time to conducting, composing, performing and teaching music. Besides completing over 400 concertos, including the famous *Le Quattro Station* (The Four Seasons), he also wrote chamber works, operas and a variety of sacred choral works.

"Laudamus te" is the second movement of Vivaldi's *Gloria*, his best known and most performed choral work. Originally set for two sopranos with an accompaniment of strings and continuo, this arrangement has been transposed down a major second and a keyboard part which is a reduction of the full orchestral score has been provided by the editor. Optional English words and dynamic indications have also been added.

This lively duet should be performed very joyously and rhythmically while always emphasizing the naturally energized syllables. The tempo should remain constant as the singers lightly sing the eighth and sixteenth note rhythmic patterns in the melismatic passages.

3. Sweet Nymph, Come to Thy Lover
Thomas Morley (c. 1557–1602) Page 24

Best known for his composition of madrigals and his development of the English madrigal, Thomas Morley was revered as a theorist, editor and organist in the Renaissance. He also composed keyboard music and music for the liturgy of the Church of England. However, it was his madrigals that made Morley famous.

Early in his career, Morley studied with William Byrd, a great Elizabethan composer of sacred music. Morley latter gave homage to his beloved teacher by dedicating to Byrd his theoretical work titled *A Plaine and Easie Introduction to Practicalle Musicke*, published in 1597. After receiving his bachelor's degree from Oxford in 1588, Morley was employed as organist at St. Paul's in London and became a Gentleman of the Chapel Royal in 1592.

Morley achieved tremendous success in the new madrigal form after he became familiar with Nicholas Yonge's publication of 1588 titled *Musica transalpina*, a collection of Italian madrigals with new English texts. Eleven collections of Morley's madrigals were published during his lifetime.

The source for this edition is *The First Booke of Canzonets to Two Voyces*, which was originally published by Thomas Este in London in 1595. This arrangement of the original "cantus" and "tenor" parts features modernized words, dynamic indications and optional keyboard and flute parts. The original has also been transposed down a major second.

Morley's canzonets were short vocal pieces meant to be performed very lightly. Although Morley wrote his many vocal pieces for a cappella ensembles, they were sometimes accompanied by viols. Instruments, such as strings, flutes or recorders, may double or replace the parts in a modern day performance. This arrangement may be performed either a cappella or with the optional keyboard and flute parts.

4. Deh prendi un dolce amplesso
Wolfgang Amadeus Mozart (1756–1791) Page 31

Wolfgang Amadeus Mozart was one of the greatest musical geniuses of all time, and his work is exemplary of the Viennese Classical style. He excelled in composing all the forms of his time, including operas, symphonies, concertos, chamber works, sonatas, choral works, arias and song. His works are highly revered today for their beautiful melodies and rich harmonies.

Born in Salzburg, Austria to a very musical family, Mozart's genius was apparent at a very early age. Concert tours with his father made Mozart a well-known performer at the piano in many European cities by his early teens. At the age of fourteen, he became concertmaster for the Archbishop of Salzburg. In 1781, against his father's advice, Mozart quit the position in Salzburg and settled in Vienna, where he spent his remaining years struggling for recognition and commissions without the security of a permanent position.

"Deh prendi un dolce amplesso" is a short duet between two men, Annio and Sesto, expressing their feelings of friendship in the first act of Mozart's last opera titled *La clemenza di Tito* (*The Clemency of Titus*), K. 621. The opera was commissioned for the coronation of Emperor Leopold II as King of Bohemia and first performed in Prague in 1791. Based on a libretto by Pietro Metastasio and revised by Caterino Mazzolà, this opera reflects on relationships, power and forgiveness while exploring the life of Roman Emperor Titus Flavius Vespasaianus. The words of this duet were added by Mazzolà.

The source of this edition is *W.A. Mozart's Sämtliche Werke*, V, published by Breitkopf and Härtel (1876–1905). Originally set for two treble voices with an accompaniment of clarinet, bassoon, horn, strings and continuo, this edition of includes a keyboard reduction of the instrumental parts. Modern clefs, dynamic and metronomic indications and optional English words have also been added by the editor.

This lilting chorus should be performed very smoothly while closely following the suggested dynamics that highlight the contrasting phrases.

94

5. Pachelbel's Canon of Peace
Johann Pachelbel (1653–1706)

Page 34

Johann Pachelbel was an outstanding German Baroque organist, composer and teacher. He studied composition and participated in instrumental performance at an early age. His first important position was that of court organist in Eisenach, the birthplace of Johann Sebastian Bach. He later worked in Nuremberg and Erfurt, where he taught Johann Christoph Bach, who eventually became the teacher of Johann Sebastian Bach. A prolific composer, he completed works for organ, harpsichord, chamber ensembles, solo vocalists and choral ensembles.

"Pachelbel's Canon of Peace" is an arrangement of the canon from the composer's best known composition, *Canon and Gigue in D Major* for three violins and basso continuo. Pachelbel originally set his canon as a chaconne, which is based both harmonically and structurally on a ground bass of eight notes. Those eight notes are repeated throughout while three violins play more complex canonic material.

This arrangement is based upon the ground bass and thematic material from the other instrumental parts and has been transposed to G major. The arranger has added tempo and dynamic indications, an optional flute part, accompaniment and text. Suitable for both school and church performance, this arrangement should be performed very smoothly to reflect the soothing nature of the words "Dona nobis pacem"—grant us peace.

This arrangement is available for performance by S.A.T.B. voices (19904), 2-part or 3-part any combination of voices (19905), and unison or 2-part voices (19906), published by Alfred Publishing Company.

6. Let's Imitate Her Notes Above
George Frideric Handel (1685–1750)

Page 40

George Frideric Handel was a very important composer of instrumental and vocal works at the end of the Baroque era. Born in Halle, Germany, he first pursued his musical career in Hamburg, playing violin in the opera house orchestra and composing his first opera, *Almira*. Handel then visited Italy in 1706 to learn the Italian style of composition, completing a number of successful operas as well as cantatas and instrumental music. He eventually settled in England to become a leading musical figure as a composer of operas and oratorios, although he wrote a number of beloved instrumental pieces, such as *Water Music*, and ceremonial church music. His large-scale oratorios in English, including many exuberant choruses for the people, made him especially popular in England. Over 3000 persons attended Handel's funeral in Westminster Abbey.

"Let's Imitate Her Notes Above" is a chorus added by Handel to the appendix of his *Alexander's Feast or The Power of Music* after he completed the original version of that work. Premiered in Covent Garden, London in 1736, this oratorio is based on an ode written by John Dryden in 1697 to celebrate St. Cecilia, the patron saint of music. Dryden's poem was later arranged by Newburgh Hamilton into a sequence of recitatives, arias, and choruses for Handel's use. The setting takes place in classical antiquity, when Alexander the Great and other characters are visited at a celebration feast by St. Cecilia. Dryden's words are an attempt to underscore the tremendous effects of music upon the emotions of humankind.

Handel personally included "Let's Imitate her Notes Above," which was set to the words of Hamilton, in his 1738 publication of *Alexander's Feast*.

The source for this edition is *Georg Friedrich Händels Werke*, Volume 12, published by Breitkopf and Härtel (1862). The original has been transposed down a minor third. Originally scored for soprano and alto voices with an accompaniment of two violins and continuo, this edition includes a keyboard part based upon the instrumental parts. Tempo and dynamic indications are further additions to Handel's original score. The original string parts are included on pages 80–85 of this publication.

7. Sonntagsmorgen
Felix Mendelssohn (1809–1847)   Page 52

In his brief life of only thirty-eight years, Felix Mendelssohn composed a great amount of music in most of the instrumental and vocal forms of his time. An esteemed musican during his lifetime, Mendelssohn traveled widely to many countries for his composing and conducting assignments. He went to England ten times and was once entertained at Buckingham Palace by Queen Victoria.

Mendelssohn's training in the music of Bach, Handel, and Mozart greatly contributed to his development as a composer. In fact, Mendelssohn is credited with revitalizing the music of Johann Sebastian Bach. When he conducted Bach's St. Matthew Passion in 1829, it was the first performance of that work since Bach's death seventy-nine years before. Mendelssohn's knowledge of the techniques and materials of past masters is evident in much of his creative output, especially in his choral works. His oratorios, particularly *St. Paul* and *Elijah*, are highly regarded for their great appeal to performers and audiences alike. His additional vocal output consists of at least one hundred-and-six lieder, thirteen vocal duets and sixty part-songs.

Completed in 1836, *"Sonntagsmorgen"* is the first of three duets in Op. 77. The original score is in E flat major for two sopranos, as provided in Mendelssohn's *Werke*, XVIII, published by Breitkopf and Härtel (1847–1877). The editor has transposed Mendelssohn's version down to C major to make the vocal parts more accessible for lower sounding voices, and a metronomic indication has been added in this publication.

Additionally, all three verses of the original German words written by Johann Ludwig Huland are provided here as well as an optional English version. Because of the sacred message of the words, this art song is also quite appropriate for church performance. The gentle mood of this selection should be rendered with a very sustained presentation of the expressive melodic lines.

8. Panis angelicus
César Franck (1822–1890)   Page 57

A renowned composer, teacher and organist in Paris, Franck was one of the most important French musicians during the second half of the nineteenth century. He was the founder of the French School, which was known for its polyphonic compositional style, and he had a profound influence upon his students.

In 1858, Franck was made organist at the church of St. Clotilde in Paris, succeeding Théodore Dubois in that post. Especially revered for his improvisation, Franck played the magnificent organ in that church until his death. He worked on his oratorio *Les Beatitudes* for over ten years and produced some of his best music in the latter portion of his life, including Sonata for Piano and Violin, Symphony in D minor, String Quartet in D Major and Three Chorales for Organ.

Franck is especially revered today for his symphonic, chamber, and keyboard works. His art songs, oratorios, masses, and other smaller vocal works have remained little known. However, his *"Panis angelicus"* is widely performed by soloists and choirs alike. Written for performance at the church of St. Clotilde, it was probably based on an improvisation which Franck played during a Christmas service in 1861. The original Latin text is the sixth verse of the Corpus Christi hymn *Sacris solemnis*. Composed as a singular work, Franck latter integrated it into his *Messa á 3 voix*.

The original version of *"Panis angelicus"* was for tenor soloist and an accompaniment of organ, harp, cello and double-bass. The work is presented here a major third lower than its original key for two voices, with optional parts for flute (or C instrument) and cello. The keyboard part provided in this arrangement is a reduction of the instrumental parts found in Franck's score.

Dynamic and tempo indications and English words have been added to this edition. This beautiful duet should be performed very legato while energizing the normally stressed syllables of the Latin or English words.

Franck's original cello part, and a flute part which is a duplication of the cello part, written two octaves higher, are on pages 86 and 87.

9. Sing with Festive Cheer
Antonio Salieri (1750–1825)   **Page 62**

Antonio Salieri was an important composer and teacher during the Classical era. Born in Italy, he first studied violin, harpsichord, thoroughbass and voice in that country before moving to Vienna. Although he traveled extensively, he eventually became a very influential musician in Vienna as the court composer and director of the Italian opera and also court Kapellmeister. Salieri received a number of honors and awards because of his successful career and participation in a number of musical organizations to promote the musical life in that city. He was also an esteemed teacher. His students included Beethoven, Schubert, Czerny, Hummel, and Liszt.

While his compositional successes included more than one hundred sacred music selections and various vocal and instrumental works, it was Salieri's more than forty operas that brought him to international acclaim. Salieri was mentored and patronized by Christoph Willibald Gluck, who encouraged Salieri to go to Paris to compose opera. Salieri's three Parisian operas between 1784 and 1787 established him as a leading operatic composer.

Salieri originally set "Sing with Festive Cheer" for two treble voices in *Les Danaides*, his first French opera which was premiered in 1784. Transposed down a minor third from the original, this arrangement includes an accompaniment based on the continuo and vocal parts. The four-measure introduction, tempo and dynamic indications, and English words have been added to this version.

This selection should be performed very energetically and rhythmically as the singers emphasize the normally stressed syllables and carefully follow the suggested dynamic changes. Rhythmic precision may be enhanced in both vocal and instrumental parts by lightly sounding the sixteenth notes which appear in succession and by slightly shortening the dotted eighth notes which are followed by sixteenth notes.

This arrangement is available for performance by S.S.A. voices (23056) and 2-part voices (23057), published by Alfred Publishing Company.

10. When at Night I Go to Sleep
Engelbert Humperdinck (1854–1921)   **Page 70**

Engelbert Humperdinck is mostly remembered today for his first opera, the beloved *Hänsel and Gretel*. Born in Siegburg, Germany, he began his musical education with piano lessons before entering the Cologne Conservatory. He excelled as a music student, winning Frankfurt's Mozart Prize in 1876, Berlin's Mendelssohn Prize in 1879 and the Meyerbeer Prize also in Berlin in 1881. When he became acquainted with Richard Wagner in Naples, Wager invited him to go to Bayreuth to assist in the production of *Parsifal*. Although he became a successful teacher at the Cologne Conservatory and latter the Hoch Conservatory in Frankfurt, Humperdinck eventually pursued his aspirations to compose operas.

In 1890, Humperdinck's sister, Adelheid Wette, asked him to assist her in creating a musical work based on two Grimm stories: *Hänsel and Gretel* and *Brüderchen und Schwesterchen (Brother and Sister)*. At first he merely provided a series of folk songs set to the texts provided by his sister Adelheid. But he later expanded his original work of music with spoken dialogue into a complete opera. Completed in 1893, Richard Strauss applauded Humperdinck's final version as a masterpiece and conducted the first performance in Weimar. The work then grew in popularity and was performed on many important stages around the world, becoming the first opera broadcast from London's Covent Garden. It has continued to remain popular for both children and adults, perhaps because of Humperdinck's use of tuneful folk melodies which are accompanied with rich orchestrations reflecting the influence of Wagner. Although Humperdinck composed six additional operas after this initial success, *Hänsel and Gretel* is his only work which is continually performed today.

This opera is about a little boy and girl who wander into the woods and get lost. During their overnight adventure, they huddle together beneath a tree and repeat their usual bedtime prayer to the "fourteen angels." The nineteenth century English translation of Constance Bache is included in this arrangement. Originally scored in D major for two treble voices with an accompaniment of flutes, oboes, clarinet, bassoons, horns and strings, this publication in C major includes a keyboard reduction of the orchestral parts. The four measure introduction, dynamic and tempo indications are additions to the original version.

This endearing duet should be performed very smoothly and freely while expressing the natural ebb and flow of the folk-like melodic lines.

Pronunciation Guides

In multiple syllable words, the syllables that should be stressed are in capital letters.

1. Ave Maria

A-ve Ma-ri-a. A-men.
AH-veh mah-RI-a. AH-mehn.

- [R] should be flipped.

2. Laudamus te *(We Praise You, Lord)*

Lau-da-mus te. Be-ne-di-ci-mus te.
lahoo-DAH-moos teh. beh-neh-DEE-chee-moos teh.

A-do-ra-mus te. Glo-ri-fi-ca-mus te.
ah-daw-RAH-moos teh. glaw-ree-fee-KAH-moos teh.

- [R] and [r] should be flipped.

4. Deh prendi un dolce amplesso *(Ah, Let Me Hold You Closely)*

Deh pren-di un dol-ce am ples-so,
deh PREHN-djoon DOHL-cheham PLEH-saw,

a-mi-co mio fe-del,
ah-MEE-kaw meeAW fay-DEHL,

e o-gnor per me lo stes-so,
ayaw-NAWR payr may law STAY-saw,

ti ser-bi a-mi-co il ciel.
tee SEHR-bjah-MEE-kaweel chehl.

- [R] and [r] should be trilled.

- [j] pronounce like the "i" in onion.

- [n] indicates that the tip of the tongue should be in contact with the lower front teeth while the front of the tongue is raised and pressed against the front of the hard palate. Nasality is then produced when breath passes through the nose, as in the Italian word "ogni"–[ohnee].

5. Pachelbel's Canon of Peace

Do-na no-bis, no-bis pa-cem.
DAW-nah NAW-bees, NAW-bees PAH-chehm.

7. Sonntagsmorgen *(This Day I Praise The Lord)*

zawn-tahks-MAWR-g<u>e</u>n

Das ist der Tag des Herrn.
d<u>a</u>s ihst dayr t<u>a</u>k dehs hehrn.

Ich bin al-lein auf wei-ter Flur.
ih<u>c</u> bihn <u>a</u>-L<u>AI</u>N <u>au</u>f V<u>AI</u>-t<u>e</u>r floor.

Noch ei-ne Mor-gen glo-cke nur,
naw<u>x</u> <u>AI</u>-n<u>e</u> MAWR-gen GLAW-k<u>e</u> noor,

nun Stil-le nah und fern.
noon SHTIH-l<u>e</u> nah oont fehrn.

An-be-tend knie' ich hier.
<u>a</u>n-BAY-t<u>e</u>nt knee i<u>c</u> heer.

O sü-ßes Grau'n! Ge-hei-mes Weh'n!
o Z<u>Y</u>:-s<u>e</u>s gr<u>au</u>n! g<u>e</u>-H<u>AI</u>-m<u>e</u>s vayn!

Als knie-ten Vie-le un-ge-seh'n und be-te-ten mit mir.
ahls KNEE-t<u>e</u>n FEE-l<u>e</u> <u>u</u>n-g<u>e</u>-ZAYN <u>u</u>nt B<u>AY</u>-t<u>e</u>-t<u>e</u>n miht meer.

Der Him-mel nah und fern, er ist so still und fei-er-lich,
dayr HIH-m<u>e</u>l nah <u>u</u>nt fehrn, ayr ihst zoh shtihl <u>u</u>nt F<u>AI</u>-er-lih<u>c</u>,

so ganz als wolt' er öff-nen sich.
zoh g<u>a</u>nts <u>a</u>ls vawlt ayr <u>O</u>F-n<u>e</u>n zih<u>c</u>.

Das ist der Tag des Herrn.
d<u>a</u>s ihst dayr t<u>a</u>k dehs hehrn.

- [<u>a</u>] (first part of) light [l<u>ai</u>ht]

- [<u>AI</u>] cr<u>y</u>, n<u>i</u>ght, p<u>ie</u>

- [<u>au</u>] ab<u>ou</u>t, h<u>ou</u>se, n<u>ow</u>

- [c] indicates that the tongue should be placed close to the palate in the position for the vowel [ee] while at the same time sharply blowing air through that opening. Known as the "ich" sound, it closely resembles the initial aspirate sound in the English word "<u>h</u>ue" that is emphasized.

- [<u>e</u>] lem<u>on</u>, ev<u>en</u>, ov<u>en</u>

- [<u>O</u>] tongue position for [eh] and lip position for [aw], as in the German word "Köpfchen"–K<u>O</u>PF-c<u>e</u>n".

- [r] and [R] should be flipped.

- [<u>u</u>] b<u>oo</u>k, l<u>oo</u>k, g<u>oo</u>d

- [<u>Y</u>] tongue position for [ee] and lip position for [oo], as in the German word "gluht"–[gl<u>y</u>t].

- [x] indicates that an aspirant, voiceless sound should be produced by blowing air to cause friction between the soft palate and the back of the tongue, which is moved up toward the soft palate, as in the German word "Ach"–[<u>a</u>x].

- [ː] indicates to lengthen the previous vowel.

8. Panis angelicus *(O Lord, I Pray to Thee)*

Pa-nis an-ge-li-cus, fit pa-nis ho-mi-num,
PAH-nees ahn-<u>DG</u>EH-lee-koos, feet PAH-nees AW-mee-noom,

Dat pa-nis coe-li-cus fi-gu-ris ter-mi-num.
daht PAH-nees CHEH-lee-koos fee-GOO-rees TEHR-mee-noom.

O res mi-ra-bi-lis man-du-cat Do-mi-num,
aw rehs mee-RAH-bee-lees mahn-DOO-kaht DAW-mee-noom,

Pau-per, pau-per, ser-vus, et hu-mi-lis,
PAHoo-pehr, PAHoo-pehr, SEHR-voos eht OO-mee-lees,

Pau-per, pau-per, ser-vus, et hu-mi-lis.
PAHoo-pehr, PAHoo-pehr, SEHR-voos eht OO-mee-lees.

- [r] should be slightly rolled when it appears at the beginning of a word and flipped when it appears between two vowels and at the end of a word.

- [<u>DG</u>] pronounce like the "j" and "dg" in the word "ju<u>dg</u>e."

10. When at Night I Go to Sleep *(Abends, will ich schlafen gehn)*

A-bends, will ich schla-fen gehn,
AH-b<u>e</u>nds, vihl ih<u>c</u> SHLAH-f<u>e</u>n gayn,

vier-zehn En-gel um mich stehn:
feer-TSAYN EH-n<u>el</u> oom mih<u>c</u> shtayn:

zwei zu mei-nen Häup-chen, wie zu mei-nen Fü-ßen,
tsv<u>ai</u> tsoo MAI-n<u>e</u>n H<u>AWY</u>P-<u>c</u>en, vee tsoo MAI-n<u>e</u>n F<u>Y</u>ː-s<u>e</u>n

zwei zu mei-ner Rech-ten, zwei zu mei-ner Lin-ken,
tsv<u>ai</u> tsoo MAI-n<u>e</u>r REH<u>C</u>-t<u>e</u>n tsv<u>ai</u> tsoo MAI-n<u>e</u>r LEEN-k<u>e</u>n,

zwei-e, die mich dek-ken, zwei-e, die mich wek-ken,
TSV<u>AI</u>-e, dee mih<u>c</u> DEH-k<u>e</u>n ZW<u>AI</u>-e, dee mih<u>c</u> WEH-k<u>e</u>n,

zwei-e, die mich wei-sen zu Him-mels Pa-ra-die-sen!
TSV<u>AI</u>-e, dee mih<u>c</u> W<u>AI</u>-z<u>e</u>n tsoo HIH-m<u>e</u>ls p<u>a</u>-r<u>a</u>-DEE -z<u>e</u>n!

- [<u>a</u>] (first part of) light [l<u>ai</u>ht]

- [<u>ai</u>] or [<u>AI</u>] cr<u>y</u>, n<u>ig</u>ht, p<u>ie</u>

- [<u>AWY</u>] Used in German, this indicates a similar sound to the English dipthong found in t<u>oy</u>, ch<u>oice</u>, j<u>oy</u>. However, in German, the second part of the dipthong [Y] is rounder than the corresponding second part in English.

- [<u>c</u>] and [<u>C</u>] indicates that the tongue should be placed close to the palate in the position for the vowel [ee] while at the same time sharply blowing air through that opening. Known as the "ich" sound, it closely resembles the initial aspirate sound in the English word "<u>h</u>ue" that is emphasized.

- [<u>e</u>] lem<u>o</u>n, ev<u>e</u>n, ov<u>e</u>n

- [<u>n</u>] si<u>ng</u>, ha<u>ng</u>, goi<u>ng</u>

- [r] and [R] should be flipped.

- [<u>Y</u>] tongue position for [ee] and lip position for [oo], as in the German word "gluht"–[gl<u>y</u>t].

- [ː] indicates to lengthen the previous vowel.